VICTOR POPOV

STATE RUSSIAN MUSEUM
LUDWIG MUSEUM IN THE RUSSIAN MUSEUM

VICTOR POPOV

MOVEMENT UPWARD

PALACE EDITIONS EUROPE

Director of the Russian Museum	Vladimir Gusyev
Editor-in-chief	Yevgenia Petrova
Artistic editor	Joseph Kiblitsky
Design	Kirill Sheverdyaev
Proofreader	Galina Maximenko
Photography	Vasily Vorontsov Petro Pelini George Popov
Translation into English	Bernhardt Grosse-Frintrop
Publisher	Joseph Kiblitsky

ISBN 3-938051-39-6 (International)

The State Russian Museum presents:
Victor Popov. Movement Upward. Almanac, Edn. 128,
Palace Editions, St Petersburg, 2005

Internet: www.rusmuseum.ru
E-mail: info@rusmuseum.ru

Printed in Italy by Graficart-Formia (LT)
Bookbindary IMAG-Cava de' Tirreni (SA)

Special thanks to Michael Sajovitz,
Gallerie Kunsthaus Oberkassel, Düsseldorf.

Contents

Victor Popov
Art, Game and Life

Visiting Victor Popov in his Düsseldorf studio turns out to be surprisingly uncomplicated and — perhaps just for this reason — an enriching thing to do: it feels as if the hundreds of paintings, reliefs, objects and sculptures stored there represent the playful side of art — not all of them, but many. Victor Popov confirms this first impression when talking about his work, which seems to be an easy thing for him, giving fulfilment and meaning to his life, not least because a large part of it has an experimental, playful character. It appears that he wants to impart the beholder something of the way he feels: the twinkle in his eye can be detected in many of his works, especially in those of the early years. And this is anything but natural, since we are facing an artist who experienced the restrictive system of the former USSR, who grew up in an atmosphere where it was opportune — to use a cautious wording — not to express a single thought, let alone painting, that would not be liked by a system keeping under lock and key not only the decisive steps of its own art history, but also and even more the substantial developments of international art.

Born in Kazakhstan, Victor Popov did his military service in the Siberian town of Semipalatinsk, the centre of Russian nuclear tests. After that he attended a painting school in Alma-Ata and finally took up a study of art at the Academy of Applied Arts in Lemberg in Western Ukraine, which he experienced as an "arrival in the centre of Europe" after his youth in the Siberian steppe, as he says. But he soon felt that the academic work was too confining and he began to represent things the way he actually perceived them. However, this was at best conformable to the academic manner demanded by his teachers, ruled by the principles of the socialist realism. His disregard of the principles that glorified the political system and the social structures not only earned him the displeasure of his teachers but finally caused him — be it by own will or for lack of opportunities — to not show his works any more in order to avoid trouble or, still more important, to avoid the risk of severe sanctions. This strategy forced by fate and shared with many unofficial artists

Play with White. 1998
Oil on wood. 23.5 x 22 cm

Recollection. 1998
Oil on wood, cardboard, paper, photo, sand. 102 x 41 x 11 cm

made him an outsider, with no chance of getting art-critical attention and passing on a personal message through his art, and all the less able to live on it: having no opportunity or permission to exhibit one's works was tantamount to staying unknown. "Everything I had learnt was now strange to me and I increasingly saw myself in the situation of finding my own style," Popov says, adding that he was always quite aware that this undertaking could prove to be extremely perilous in the USSR in the 1970s (when he started developing his own style).

Especially while in St. Petersburg, where he stayed sporadically from 1971 and permanently from 1984, until his emigration to Germany in 1991, he consistently pursued his own goals. It was there that he developed a very individual style, which included both fantastic-realistic components and elements of caricature — a figurative artistic expression sometimes marked by black humour. Until the 1990s, human beings were at the centre of his works, and this is so at present, although in a more subtle, cryptic way.

"My heroes were in no way simple personalities, but leaders and wise men who dreamt of ruling people and preaching the truth. But in view of such aspirations always being in a way doubtful, my characters had comical traits," he says about his work during that period. Even without his characters being presented in a portrait-like style and considering the circumstance that Popov had a distant attitude towards the historic facts, especially towards the Soviet political scene, the beholder understands the statement behind the overdrawn figures he laid in a world between bizarre theatre and grotesque; involved in scenes with partly an obscene touch, it is a symbolic setting representing a society whose civil individuals were maltreated with dubious values and norms.

Popov's attitude towards his own creative activity is surprisingly dissociated, much of it being "too academic" in his eyes, although the term "academic" at most applies to the aesthetic design — the notion of figure and space prevailing in his works, the remaining levels showing such a great deal of irony, sarcasm and ambiguity that his representational artworks were destined to meet with the displeasure of the art functionaries of the former USSR.

But Victor Popov's art world is not merely a figurative one. Over the years, he gradually moved away from the narrative scenario, adopting a more abstract formal style, experimenting with materials, techniques and style elements that are known from the Russian avant-garde of the early twentieth century, as well as Western European classical modernity. Only when he came to the West did the artist became acquainted with a wealth of originals he had been able to view at best secretly in Russia as reproductions in (prohibited) books and catalogues with friends from the intellectual, non-conformist St. Petersburg scene.

In the late 1990s, there seemed to be an albeit temporary break with the figurative style of art. This was a time when Popov created compositions, mostly out of wood, such as *Play with White* (1998), *White Point* (1998), *Secret* (1998) or *Recollection* (1998). Popov chooses titles for his works which either take up the immediately visible or put the beholder on its track by means of abstract notions, not giving him any clue to interpretation. The coloration of these compositions is often discreet; they are relief-style collages presenting a notable synthesis of painting and sculpture. These coarse works also reveal the craftsman's side of Victor Popov, who thought out and manufactured gymnastic and playing apparatuses for public playgrounds for many years to earn a living: a common practice among those artists who did not see their vocation in fulfilling the doctrine of socialist realism or in forms moderated to suit the official art ideology. Here, as in other picture works showing this constructivist note, we find an artist approaching and about to get attached to the Russian avant-garde, reflecting its formal language and transferring it into the present: names like Ivan Puni, Vasily Ermilov, Ivan Kliun or Nikolai Suetin are evoked. Victor Popov's change from the humoristic, ironic tenor to a comparatively serious way of dealing with the cultural-historical heritage of his native country seems like a confession that became necessary in a foreign country and is coupled to an emigrant's working out of his own identity. Popov has felt an

White Point. 1998
Oil on canvas. 25 x 32 cm

Secret. 1998
Oil on metal, paper
103 x 41 x 9 cm

Factory (Red). 2000
Oil on wood. 64 x 75.5 x 17 cm

emotional link to his native land until today: "I've been continuing my experiments in Germany meanwhile, to be more exact in the Eifel, its landscape reminding me of my home in the foothills of the Altai mountains."

Another group of works consists of wooden objects, which are often monotone and mostly medium sized, being experiments with the effect of form and colour. Representative examples covering more or less the thematic spectrum of this type of three-dimensional objects are *Factory (Red)* (2000), *Desire* (2001), *Head* (2004) and *Yellow Object* (2000). Some of them refer to a concrete object, yet not depicting it (*Factory (Red), Head*). Some have abstract terms as a title, embodying frames of mind in a similar way as *Recollection*. Erotic desire is expressed here also by the formal language, building a bridge to one of the pictorial ten-

Excitement. 2001
Acrylic on plywood. 82 x 54 x 12 cm

Yellow Object. 2000
Acrylic on plywood. 149 x 61 x 18 cm

Head. 2004
Acrylic on plywood. 98 x 77 x 21 cm

Composition No. 77. 2002
Oil on canvas. 77 x 66 cm

Composition White on Yellow. 2002
Oil on canvas. 80 x 65 cm

dencies of former years. Ultimately, there is a great number of totally abstract objects — quasi three-dimensional counterparts of such painted variants as *Composition No. 77* (2002) and *Composition White on Yellow* (2002). Here the two-dimensional composition fakes three-dimensionality, as the reliefs recall paintings, by being seemingly two-dimensional, through a form borrowed from Suprematism.

A tenor embracing all the works is the gambling theme, most explicitly represented by the "dice paintings": *Game with Yellow Dice* (2002), *Game on Black Square* (2002) or *Game — Queen of Spades* (2002). The dice, the symbol of the game, is a central element found at least once in each of these picture variants in a consistently naïve stereo-metrical conception, with a distorted perspective, showing one or three spots. As a shape, it has a correlation to other basic geometric shapes such as the circle, rectangle or cross — all of which contain one or even various symbolic meanings. The black square, for instance, has become the symbol of Suprematism and something similar is true of the cross, making it more than a Christian sign. Analogously, the interpretative levels of Victor Popov's art are crossed in a very graphic way in *Flight of the*

Game — Queen of Spades. 2002
Oil on canvas. 96 x 69 cm

Game with Yellow Dice. 2002
Oil on canvas. 80 x 65 cm

Game on Black Square. 2002
Oil on canvas. 80 x 65 cm

Dices (2004) and *Untitled* (2004). Just as *Game on Black Square* is an unmistakable homage to the *Black Square* of Kazimir Malevich, *Flight of the Dices* takes up the cosmic aspect, which is very typical of Russian art, also playing a decisive role in Suprematism. At the same time, this type of painting is about gambling as such with all its unpredictability.

Being an optimist full of humour, Victor Popov imagines life ideally as a game, where there are neither winners nor losers, or rather where the winner is a loser and the loser is a winner. His artistic existence, the way he understands it, is one of countless forms of existence on a large playing field, which are all possible and justified, everybody having his or her own place. In the world of art, he sees himself as someone who goes his own way, both when he lived in the Soviet Union as well as today in the West. The mainstream is not interesting to him, he prefers to rely on his intuition: "Of course I also want to find some truth; but I trust more in the material, the work and the artist's instinct than in any sophisticated products of intellect."

Victor Popov does not regard himself as an artist whose work may be approachable to intellectual circles at best, but as a man whose fate has determined him to be creative. His work reflects the way he feels about life: a game in which happiness and unhappiness, gain and loss, are the result of chance and your own attitude.

Dr. Barbara M. Thiemann

Victor Popov's Colourplastics

At the *Abstraction in Russia: XX Century* exhibition held at the State Russian Museum in 2001, the work of Victor Popov was displayed in a special area, closing the whole enfilade of the exhibition halls. The exhibition holders were governed by quite objective circumstances: Popov's object three-dimensional *Yellow* (wood, glue, primer, oil) had apparent space-making qualities. Among a host of non-figurative works of art (this exposition was remarkable for a special representation), he was chosen exactly because he was able to confidently keep this complex space, consisting of many parts penetrated with variously directed energies. Well-timbered (in this case the expression, which has already become a metaphor, has a literal sense — a plan of an engineering implementation) and holding tenaciously space by its sharp faces, attracting by its non-compromise objectivistic colour with no shading, it had the abilities of some independent life, accented presence, i.e. qualities which according to the associate of one of the classics of non-figurative art, Hans Arp, the personalities of the European vanguard were looking for in non-figurativeness: "He (Arp) wanted immediate products... A kind of a theroid creature with the primitive tension and jazz. A new body near us, which lives by itself... He wanted abstraction."

The culture of the object, and then an assembly thinking, which Victor Popov has developed successfully in recent years, undoubtedly originates from the Cubo-Futurist tradition, transformed to a great extent by Suprematism and Constructionism. Or, more exactly from its collective image, which is hardly reflected by him from the purely art history and historic-stage viewpoint. I would say pre-artistic, personal experience of Popov has influenced the classics of non-figurativeness, the works of this kind not to a lesser degree than allusions. Admittedly, he was already an artist, completed a training when he was getting such experience. However, he, for certain, did not think about its application in grand art as well as about his own future work in the context of an abstract art. I mean that page of Popov's biography, even more employment, and not an artistic biography, when he

Flight of the Dices. 2004
Oil on canvas. 120 x 100 cm

Untitled. 2004
Oil on canvas. 120 x 100 cm

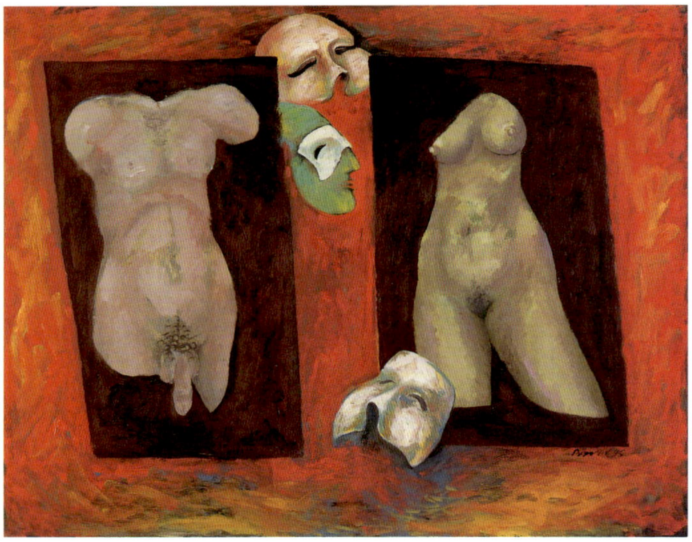

Untitled. 1995
Oil on canvas. 110 x 90 cm

Torso and Purple. 1994
Oil on canvas. 100 x 80 cm

travelled throughout Russia, earning money by designing children's playgrounds. In the context of the Soviet ideas about high art, this activity was undoubtedly craft-like and profane-like. However, I believe this experience was very important for the future development of Popov. Osip Mandelstam created a remarkable image: "the grasping eye of a simple carpenter." This is exactly what I mean: some immediate, tactile, bodily experience of contact with material — wood, space, and lastly with a game. All this found its continuation in due time...

But first, a few words about his background.
Victor Popov was born in 1952 in the East of Kazakhstan, in a small town found in the foothills of the Altai mountains. He travelled from one end of the country to the other — Semipalatinsk, Alma-Ata where he got his first classes in drawing, and finally Western Ukraine, Lvov, the Institute of Decorative and Applied Art where he studied from 1974 to 1979. Popov failed to be a diligent student. Unsatisfied with the system of education, he took to the road again. His work related to designing children's playgrounds is exactly from this period and the first contact with wood as a material. He felt an independent artist in St. Petersburg only, Leningrad then, where he moved in the 1980s. It was the period of the decay of semi-official and mass, albeit mediated by non-personal experience, publications and albums, access to Western art: the artists at large (and not only chosen people — dissidents as it used to be) opened new horizons for themselves. Expressionist and Surrealist traditions became such horizons for many. In Leningrad, a local version of Surrealism was created by a large group of artists; its experience was reduced to some collective image, eased and ultra literary centric. They formed a few artistic unions, the *Island* union probably being the most influential. Popov exhibited readily with the *Island* union of artists, sharing both their sincerity of aspirations and their language, which was a kind of typological, beyond individualization. Apparently, it seemed for him that exactly this language — a language of enhanced expression (and respective references to classics of an expressive line of the world art from Bosch to Grosse) accelerated literature attributes and methods of various kind of Surrealist sug-

gestibility was the only possible form to express those moods which the artist felt. Moods, which were eschatological, related to the ruining of the accustomed everyday life and public ties connected with the decay of the USSR. What could be done, many shared Popov's feelings, many started to use the same sources, hence the common vulnerable moments first of all connected with the secondary and undistinguished language. And still this stage in the development of Popov continued further in the next decade (from 1991 the artist lived only in Germany) is very important. And not only because several serious works left after it: just less heart-rending, objectified in terms of pictorial implementation — *Untitled* (1995), *Torso and Purple* (1994) and *Seduced Woman* (1995). I think Popov found his sense of freedom during this period. He does not hide allusions to poetics of masters close to him, not forgetting to mention their names in the titles to such paintings as *Still-Life with Jawlensky* and *Landscape with Leger*, i.e. he does not 'study' the material of 'other people's' art in the school meaning of this term, he doesn't appropriate other people's experience, and more so he doesn't copy. He reacts to experience of great predecessors in a mobile, lively and even playing manner. And it means that he gets rid of that bitter-end that let down his many ex-associates who stayed loyal to the Leningrad version of Surrealism, he got a chance to look at his art as if onlooking. And began his next stage by a kind of return to own, not conceptualized until then in the context of art experience — work experience with wood. From the second half of the 1990s he began to make wooden sculptures — totems. A reflection on that line of a modernist tradition which was oriented to organic, more often primitivizing type of culture — traditions of Brancusi, Moore and Giacometti is obvious in them. And along with that as though a layer deeper of this cultural memory another memory — memory of hands, carpentry memory, memory of work with small, but space of the children's playground open wide towards outside. I believe that an accented feeling of hand made and looking through of this sculpture comes from this memory, activated and reflected in a new situation — situation of through frames, slots, work for transmitted light, etc. I'd like to specially emphasize the mo-

Seduced Woman. 1995
Oil on canvas. 75 x 90 cm

Still-Life with Jawlensky. 1996
Oil on canvas. 120 x 100 cm

Landscape with Leger. 1996
Oil on canvas. 120 x 100 cm

Red Triangle. 2003
Acrylic on plywood. 76 x 76 x 15 cm

ment of such hand-made: this is exactly hand-made articulation, it is important to demonstrate for him how wood is soft to him and this unsophisticated confidence in his power of the carver, material processor undoubtedly tint the form-making.

In my view, the tendency of a total release from mimetic has become the most significant stage, in fact it continues until now: Popov creates a series of powerful, well timbered wooden objects running to pure geometry. They are totally lack of pictorialism in the mimetic sense of word, it seems that they are fully in line with the formula of the theoretician of the Russian Constructivism Nikolai Tarabukin: a form of a piece of art develops from two major moments — material and construction due to which a material is organized into a completed whole gaining its completed logic and internal sense. It seems that Popov goes a classic way of the Russian vanguard. What new can be found on this way? In very deed it is not simple to drive own stakes in this area. That is probably why there are not so many masters in actual fact consistently developing a geometric project: one can remember V. Koleichuk, F. Infante, L. Borissov, and a couple other names.

And still Popov, I think, has found this personal area. And the matter is not only that his geometry is a crossing and truncation of geometric forms, new methods for their coupling and interference, activation of space-making properties — rarely independent and inventive. First of all, undoubtedly he rests on the practice of Suprematism-Constructivism (as if he proposed own passwords intended for entry into these topics, for example, in the object of 2002 *'Red Triangle'*) he adds new elements to this discourse. As if he entered — I don't know whether after reflection or intuitively — a certain dialogue with a later art practice, which in its turn entered with the Russian vanguard in relations of piety-polemics in due time. I mean the concrete art practice not losing its topicality for many decades. Theo van Doesburg in 1930 in

Paris published the *Art Concrete* manifesto, where he declared: 'A piece of art... does not borrow anything from natural forms, or contain anything sensible or sentimental... Technique, implementation should be mechanistic, in other words, anti-impressionistic.' Since then, this line, especially typical of a post-war, European generation of artists, draws the map of art of both Western, and Eastern Europe. And Popov allows himself to debate with this influential line of totally independent, all-sufficient, not interested in any figurative references and symbolic associations of arts. First of all, moments, which are fundamental for *Art Concrete* that is relation to non-manual, machine form and "mechanical" composition technique — repeat, motifs, etc. In Popov's space compositions exactly machine and mechanical — its geometry is another, hand-made, often "irregular": the line is drawn (carved, cut) by hand and therefore it may shake and vibrate, planes and dimensions are not ground in with machine-like manufacturability, hence — plays and slots, which all of sudden begin to play own parts. Finally, colour: despite Doesburg's postulate his 'technique and implementation' are far from being mechanistic-like and even emotional. Well-timbered under influence of certain centrifugal forces or on the contrary ready to "fly apart" into elements under influence of centripetal force, its objects are not also free from "natural associations" (the one, which the follower of Doesburg M. Bill disliked so and who postulated a refusal from "naturalistic representations," radical emancipation from "natural"). Admittedly, these associations are not naturalistic, but mostly internal, esoteric sense. Well, same N. Tarabukin wrote that "pure" forms released from pictorialism begin already at the moment of this release still to "express" at a new stage their peculiar reality. I can't, but give one more quotation: "reality only begins when its objects end (H. Ball)." However such object art (it is meant so-called real object art, i.e. natural, produced articles, things) is also close to Popov. In parallel with non-figurative space objects he creates assemblies, in effect, found-objects as real "found" objects such as children's dolls, telephone, reproduction, palette, etc. are involved in it. The artist satisfies his passion for a story, narration this way, and it is hardly something may be more narrative than the objects which have done their time... This is how the creativity of Popov develops, and along with objects and assemblies he continues to paint: between the poles of "pure" form-making and narration. And as it is known energy originates between the poles. The best works of Victor Popov — and I include there first of all his non-figurative objects — have the energy of presence in its kind. They present not only at the exhibition halls, but in the mind of a looker, in his memory.

Alexander Borovsky

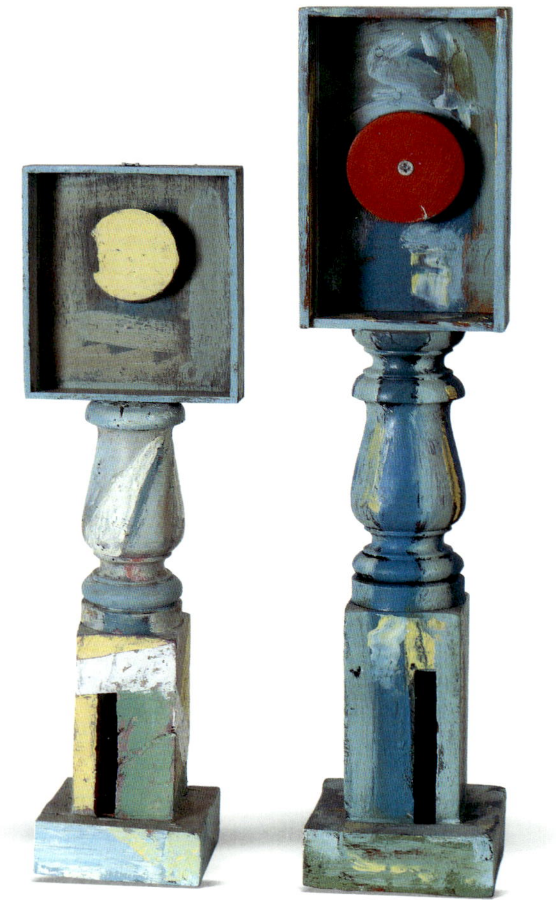

Yellow and Red Post. 2001
2 parts. Oil on canvas
52 x 11.4 x 10 cm & 43 x 12 x 9.6 cm

COLOUR PLATES

Composition 3D. 1996
Oil on canvas. 80 x 95 cm

Black-White Portrait. 52 prs. 1999
Acrylic on cardboard, wax. 30 x 23 cm

Composition No. 82. 2001
Oil on wood, canvas. 54 x 65.5 cm

Window. 1998
Oil on canvas, wood, paper. 78 x 94 cm

A Play With a Brick on the
Green Background. 2002
Oil on canvas. 100 x 90 cm

On the Red Table. 2002
Oil on canvas. 120 x 100 cm

Composition No. 23. 2002
Oil on canvas. 99 x 74 cm

Composition the
White-Blue. 2002
Oil on canvas. 80 x 65 cm

Aggressive Head. 2002
Oil on canvas. 100 x 90 cm

Composition No. 2 (Mess). 2002
Oil on canvas. 100 x 90 cm

Composition 4 with Bricks
on the Grey Background. 2002
Oil on canvas. 120 x 100 cm

NNO 1994

Untitled. 1998
Oil on wood, paper. 55 x 54 cm

100% Tobacco. 1998
Oil on wood, paper. 55 x 54 cm

Box. 1998
Oil on wood, metal, paper
29 x 80 x 10 cm

hts wert'

Jesus. 1999
Oil on canvas, wood,
cardboard. 84 x 43 cm

Movement Upward. 1998
Oil on wood, metal. 170 x 46 x 4 cm

Knight. 1998
Oil on wood, metal, paper
120 x 52 x 7 cm

Untitled (Watch). 2003
Oil on wood, metal
109 x 48 cm

Untitled. 2002
Oil on plywood, cardboard
100 x 59 x 13 cm

Untitled. 2000
Oil on wood, paper, metal, leather
95 x 44 cm

Red Point. 1999
Oil on wood
57 x 47.5 cm

Window. 1998
Oil on plywood, paper, cardboard
68 x 48 x 9 cm

Humazh on Music. 2003
Oil on acrylic, wood, metal, paper
123 x 60 x 32 cm

Orange. 2001
Oil on wood, plywood
91 x 43 x 18 cm

Futuristic Portrait. 2003
Acrylic on plywood
78 x 50 x 11 cm

Wing. 2000
Acrylic on plywood. 63.5 x 54.5 x 13 cm

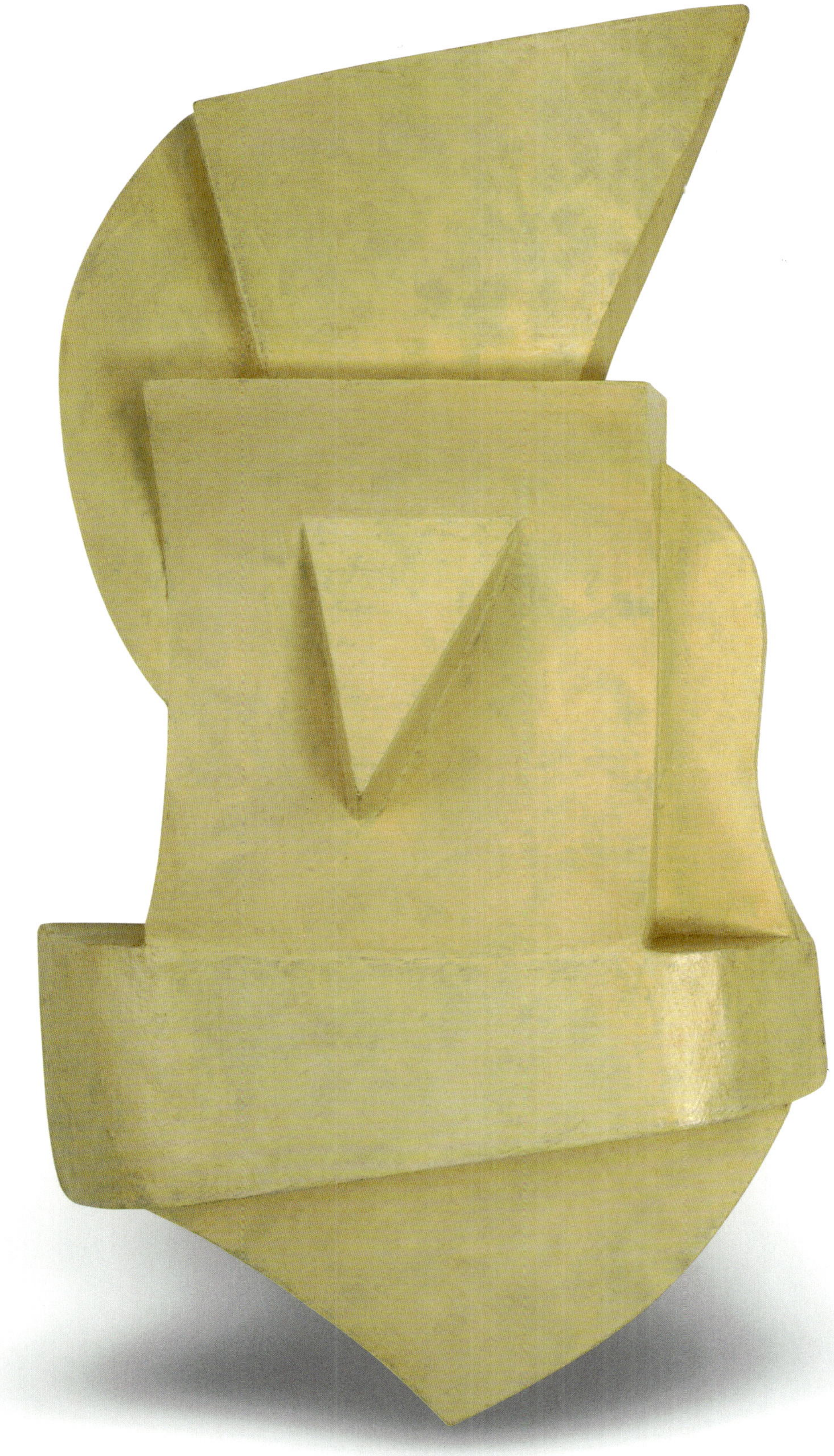

Untitled. 2001
Oil on plywood. 74 x 40 x 12 cm

Red. 2002
Acrylic on wood, plywood. 92 x 51 x 12 cm

Golden Autumn. 2002
Acrylic on wood. 89 x 41 x 13 cm

The River in Autumn. 2002
Acrylic on wood. 34 x 73 x 13 cm

Red. 2002
Oil on plywood, acrylic
166 x 68 x 7 cm

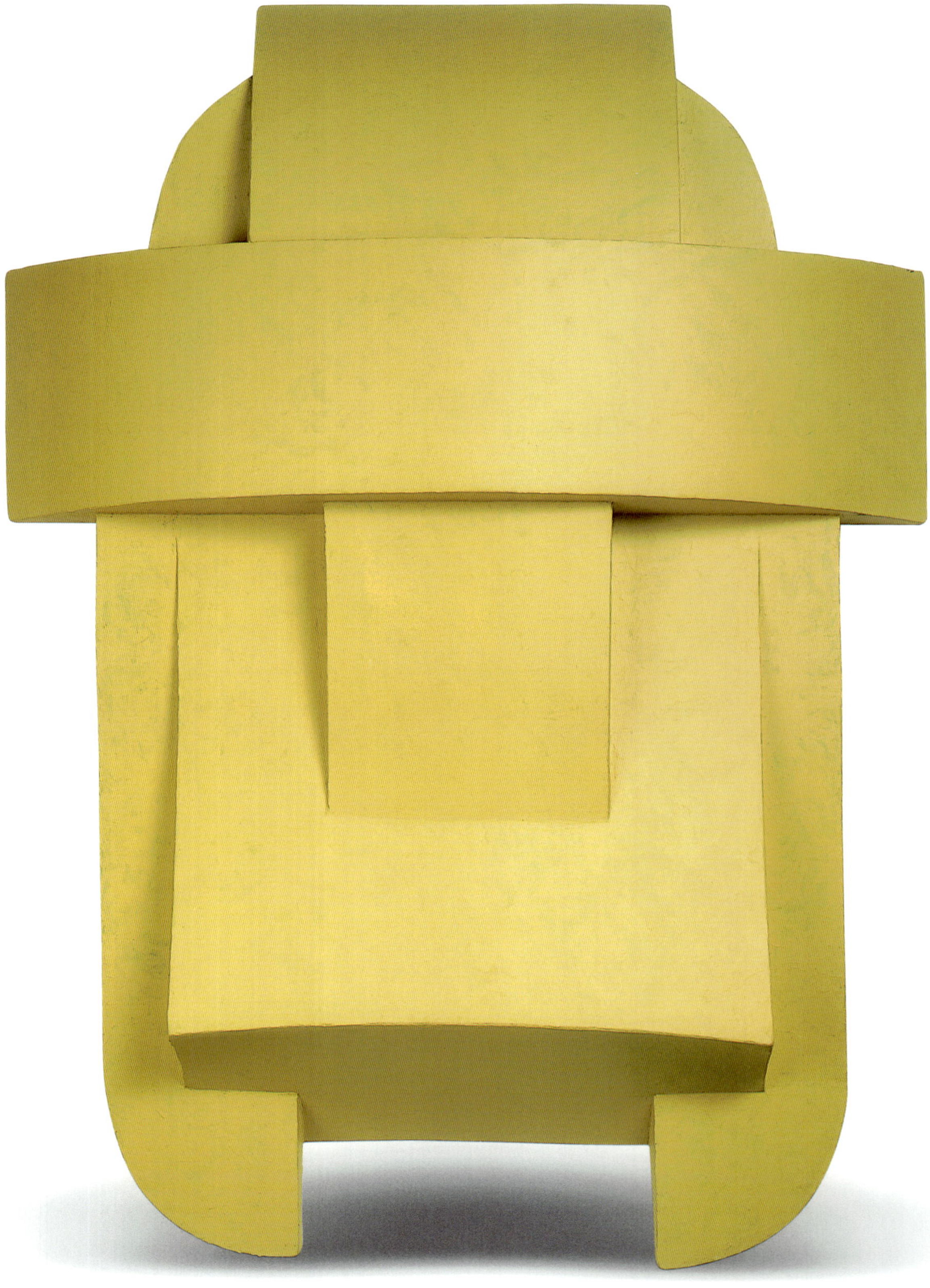

Man Geometry. 2003
Acrylic on plywood. 110 x 77 x 16 cm

Head No. 2. 2003
Acrylic on plywood. 72 x 53 x 10 cm

Rainbow. 2003
Acrylic on plywood. 104 x 65 x 17 cm

Movement of the Black Triangle. 2002
Acrylic on plywood. 107 x 55 x 16 cm

An Eye. 2003
Acrylic on plywood. 76 x 76 x 17 cm

Blue Object. 2002
Oil on plyboard. 43 x 97 x 9 cm

Yellow Factory. 2001
Oil on wood. 51 x 93 x 14 cm

White Object. 2002
Oil on plyboard. 51.5 x 91 x 13 cm

Untitled. 2002
Acrylic on plywood. 176 x 90 x 27 cm

Untitled. 2000
Oil on plywood. 63 x 58 x 15 cm

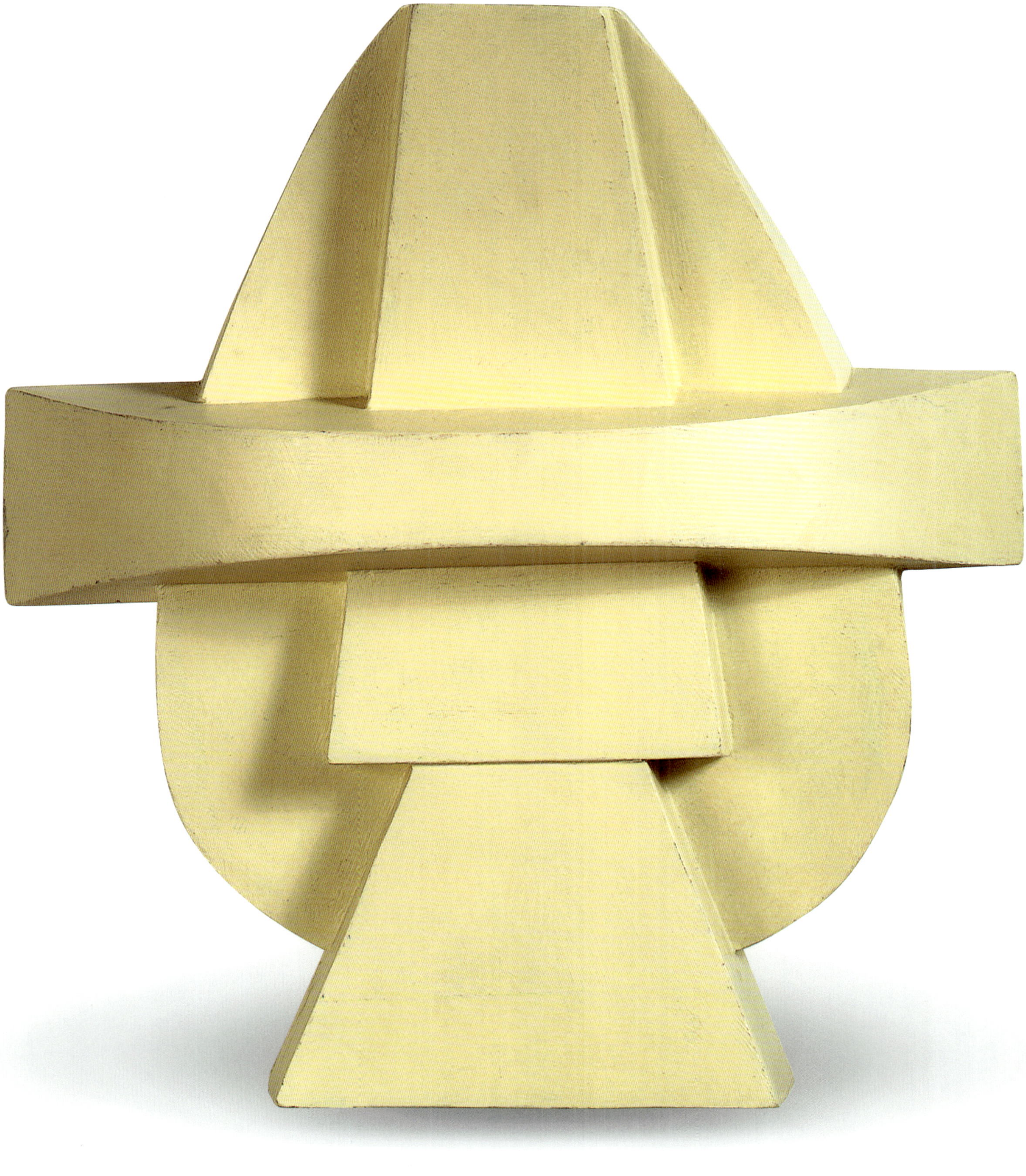

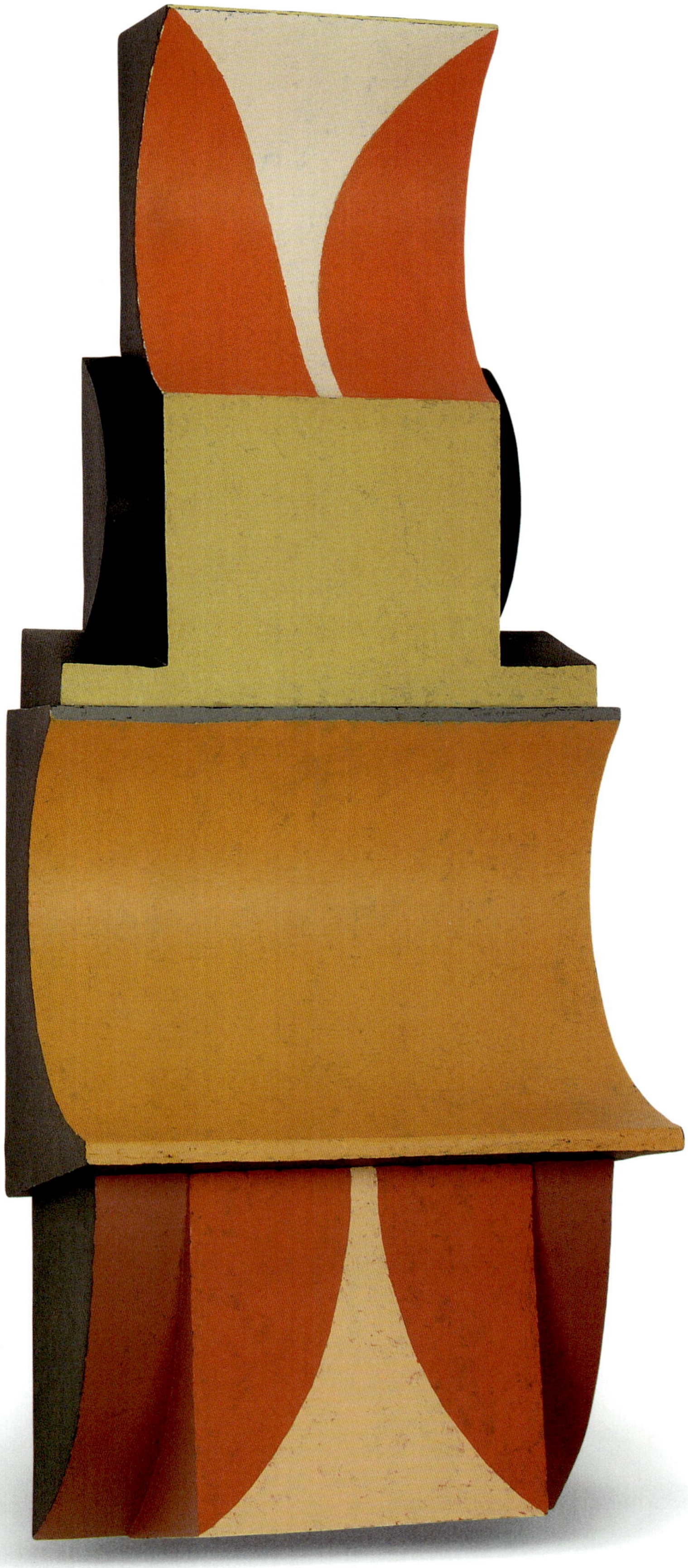

Untitled. 2003
Acrylic on plywood. 147 x 55 x 30 cm

Untitled. 2002
Oil on playwood. 65 x 32 x 9.5 cm

BAUHAUS
BAUHAUS

One "X". 2004
Acrylic on plywood. 76 x 76 x 15 cm

Movement in a Square. 2004
Acrylic on plywood. 76 x 76 x 15 cm

Movement on the White Background. 2004
Acrylic on plywood. 76 x 76 x 15 cm

Beginning of Movement. 2002
Acrylic on plywood. 76 x 76 x 13 cm

Yellow in a Square. 2003
Acrylic on plywood. 76 x 76 x 10 cm

Untitled. 2002
Acrylic on plywood. 76 x 76 x 11 cm

Swimming Tree. 2003
Acrylic on wood, plywood. 76 x 76 x 13 cm

Sunrise. 2003
Acrylic on plywood. 76 x 76 x 13 cm

White in a Yellow-Black Square. 2003
Acrylic on plyboard. 76 x 76 x 16 cm

Yellow-Grey Triangle on the
Red-White Background. 2004
Acrylic on plywood. 76 x 76 x 19 cm

Yellow. Red. White. 2003
Acrylic on plywood.76 x 76 x 15 cm

Washing-Board. 2005
Acrylic on plywood, metal. 103 x 78 x 13 cm

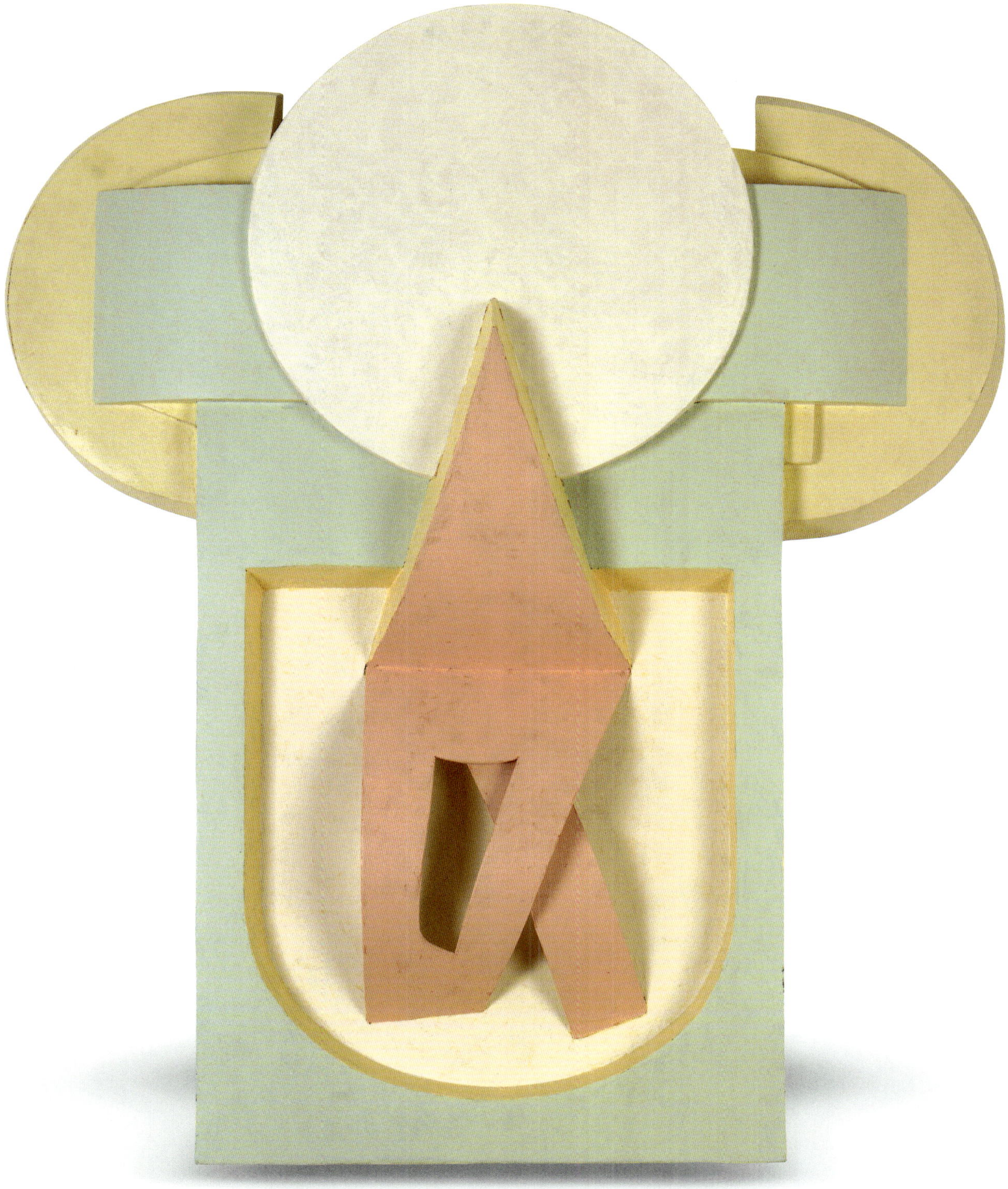

Untitled. 2003
Acrylic on plywood. 116 x 90 x 17 cm

Red No. 2. 2005
Oil on plywood. 96 x 77 x 17 cm

Color

Untitled. 2003
Acrylic on plywood. 28 x 65 cm

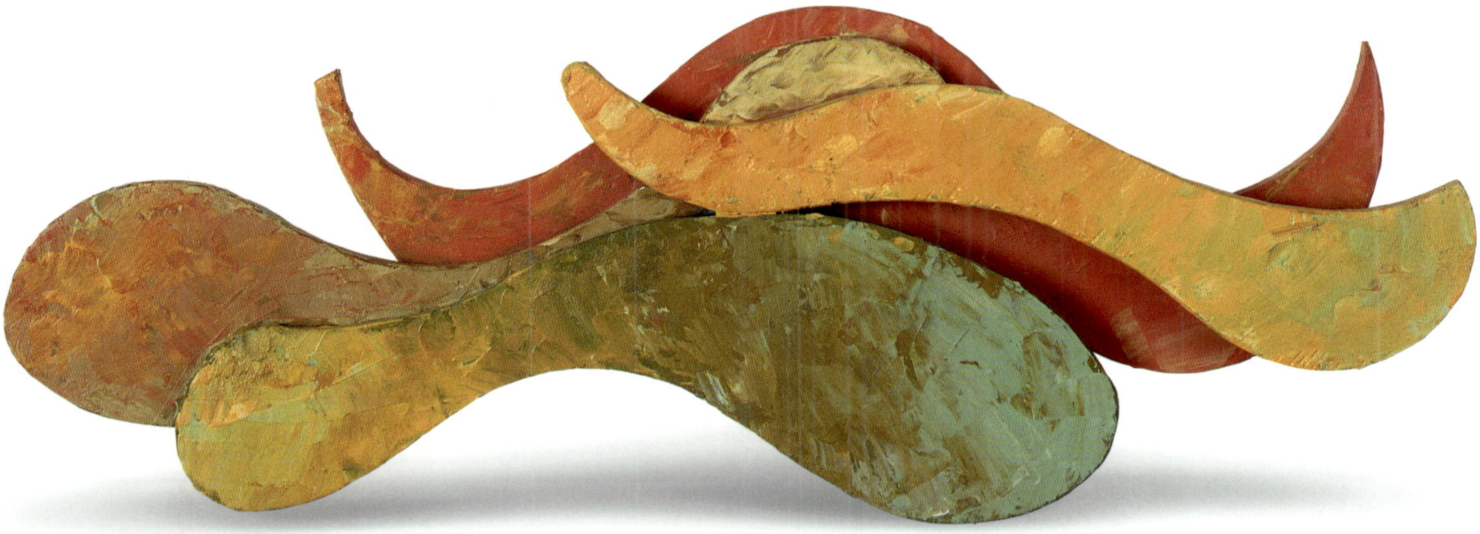

Composition No. 7. 2003
Acrylic on plywood. 20 x 54 cm

Composition No. 8. 2004
Acrylic on plywood. 28 x 82 cm

Composition No. 9. 2003
Acrylic on plywood. 44 x 20 cm

Red Sailing Vessel. 2003
Acrylic on plywood. 31 x 50.5 cm

Blue Sailing Vessel. 2003
Acrylic on plywood. 45 x 23 cm

Sailing Vessel. 2003
Acrylic on plywood. 54 x 30 cm

Untitled. 2004
Acrylic on plywood. 31 x 50 cm

Untitled. 2004
Acrylic on plywood. 25 x 48 cm

Untitled. 2004
Acrylic on plywood. 116 x 55 x 27 cm

Untitled. 2001
Oil on plywood. 82 x 43 x 20 cm

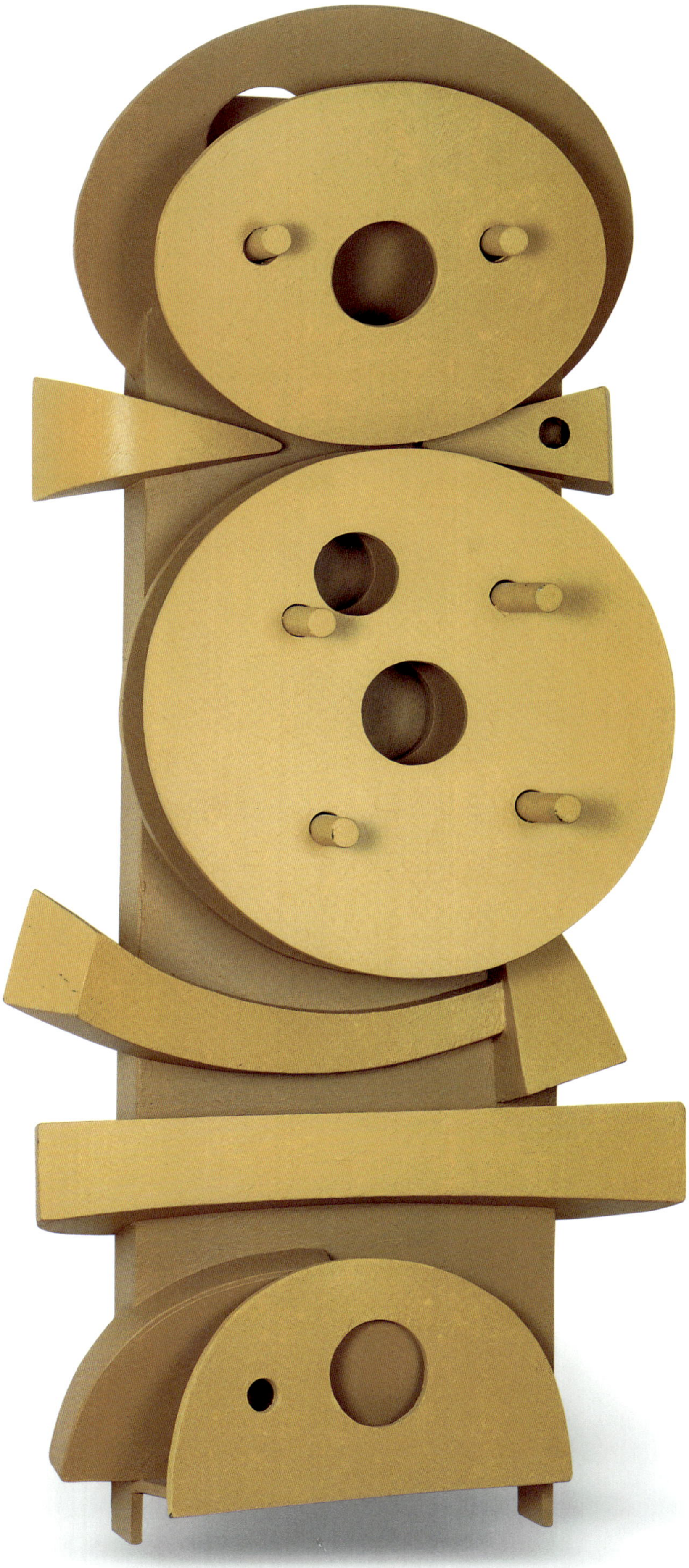

Untitled (Yellow). 2004
Acrylic on plywood. 159 x 72 x 28 cm

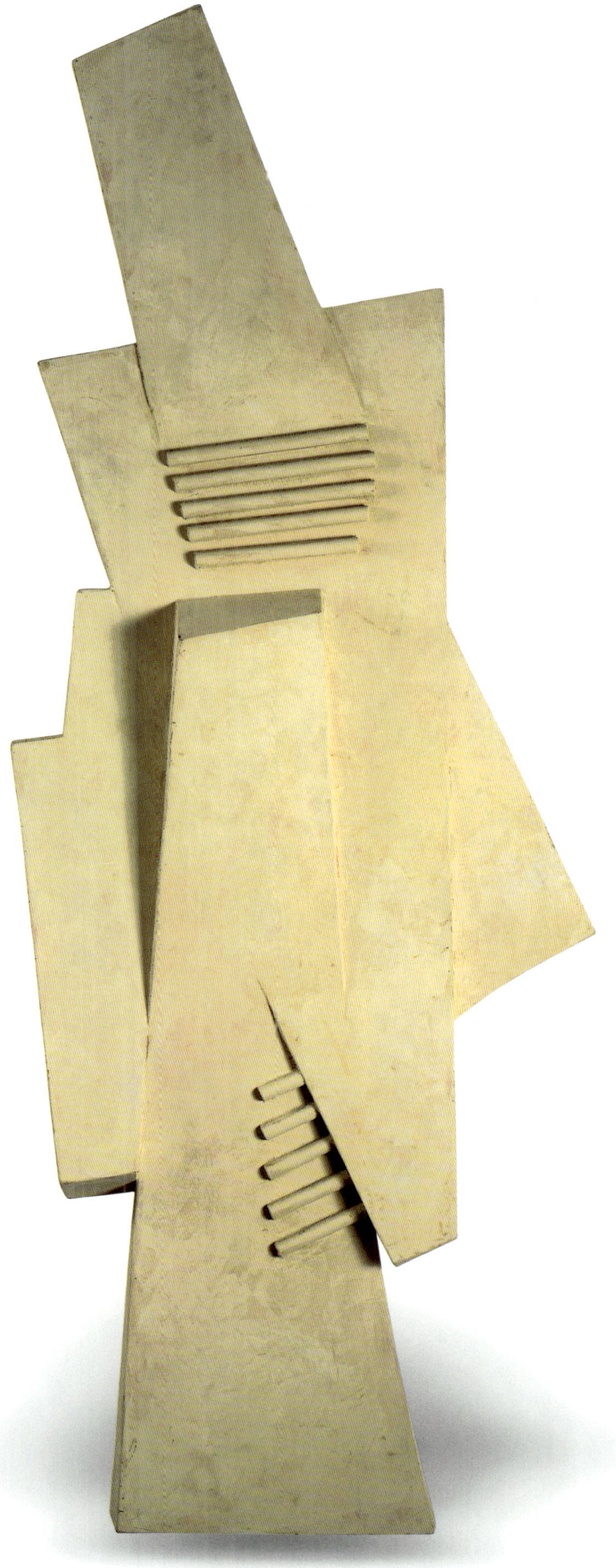

Musical. 2002
Acrylic on plywood. 155 x 55.5 cm

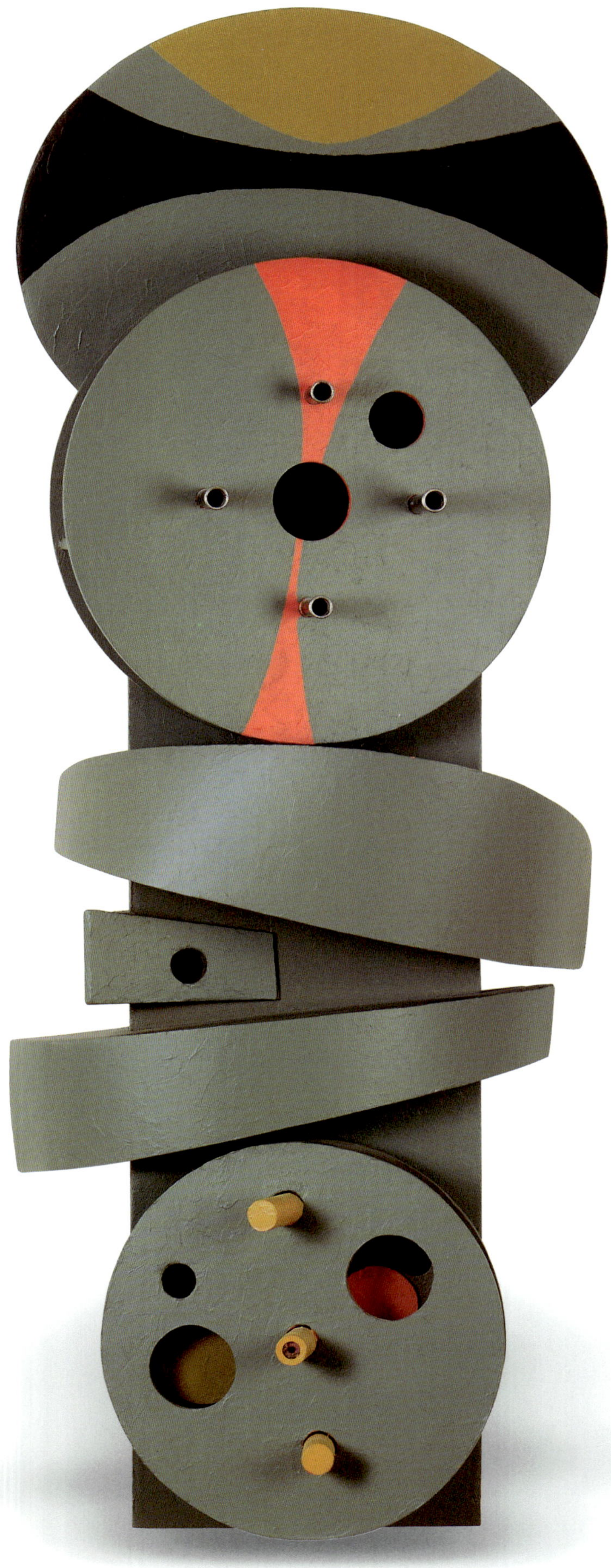

Untitled. 2004
Acrylic on plywood, metal
162 x 61 x 27 cm

Untitled. 2004
Acrylic on plywood
79 x 61 x 17 cm

Black Chair with a Telephone. 2004
Oil on wood, telephone. 86 x 42 x 43 cm

Red Chair with a Telephone. 2004
Oil on wood, telephone. 84 x 46 x 44 cm

Napoleon. 2003
Acrylic on plywood. 177 x 41 x 52 cm

Untitled. 2003
Acrylic on plywood. 176 x 42 x 54 cm

Checkmate. 2002
Acrylic on wood. 179 x 36 x 36 cm

People in space

Sculpture. 1996
Wax on Wood. 190 x 42 cm

Sculpture. 1996
Wax on Wood. 230 x 44 cm

Sculpture. 1997
Wax on Wood. 188 x 34 cm

Sculpture. 1996
Wax on Wood. 196 x 28 cm

Victor Popov was born in the Eastern part of Kazakhstan in 1952. He studied at the Lvov Institute of Applied Art (Ukraine). Since 1980 Victor Popov has been a freelance artist. The subject of his works was Children Playgrounds. Victor Popov has contributed to numerous exhibitions in the art galleries and museums of Russia, Germany, Korea, Japan, Sweden, France and Montenegro. From 1991 the artist lives and works in Dusseldorf, Germany.

Major museum exhibitions:

City History Museum, St. Petersburg
Seoul, South Korea
State Russian Museum, St. Petersburg
Museum für Kunst, Nordhaisen
Tivot City Museum, Montenegro